Dana Perino New

Book 2025

Practical Wisdom for Achieving

Success, Resilience, and Meaning

Copyright © 2025

Table of Contents

Introduction

The Journey to Meaningful Success

We all want success. But what does success really mean? To some, it's climbing the corporate ladder, earning a prestigious title, or achieving financial freedom. For others, success is finding balance between their career and personal life, nurturing meaningful relationships, or simply waking up each day with a sense of purpose.

The truth is, success is personal. It's not a one-size-fits-all formula, and it certainly doesn't happen overnight. But the journey toward success doesn't have to feel like a long, lonely road. Along the way, we can rely on a treasure trove of wisdom from those who've walked similar paths. If we open ourselves to learning, adapt along the way, and embrace the lessons life has to offer, we can shape our own version of success.

This book is about that journey—the one where you build your career and your life with intention, mindfulness, and the guidance of those who have gone before you. It's about understanding that every step you take, even the missteps, is part of a greater story. And most importantly, it's about recognizing that the road ahead is yours to create, but it doesn't hurt to have a map.

Why Advice Matters and How to Use It

Throughout my career, I've been lucky to have had mentors and advisors who shared their hard-earned wisdom with me. Some lessons were gentle nudges in the right direction, while others were wake-up calls that shook me out of complacency. Some advice came from people I worked with, some from family and friends, and some from unexpected sources. Regardless of where it came from, all of it had one thing in common: it shaped my thinking and, ultimately, my choices.

But here's the thing about advice—it's only helpful if you're willing to take it in, reflect on it, and apply it to your own life. It's easy to listen and nod, but real growth happens when you put the advice into action. The trick is learning how to sift through the noise and find the nuggets that truly resonate with your goals, values, and aspirations. Not every piece of advice will be right for you, but when you find the ones that are, they can become your guiding stars.

In this book, I'll share with you the best advice I've received, along with insights from my mentors and colleagues, all of whom have built meaningful careers and lives of their own. Some of the lessons may surprise you, others may seem like common sense, but all are designed to help you navigate the challenges you'll face as you build your own version of success.

So, as you read these pages, keep an open mind, and take the advice that feels right for you. Whether you're just starting out or looking to make a change, the journey to meaningful success is a continual process of learning, growing, and refining your path. And remember—while success is personal, you don't have to go it alone.

Let's get started.

Chapter One

Foundations of a Great Career

Building a great career isn't about luck or timing alone. It's about understanding yourself, having a clear vision, and putting in the hard work day in and day out. In this chapter, we'll dive into the foundational elements that set the stage for long-term success, from discovering your passion to setting goals and cultivating persistence. These elements will serve as the bedrock upon which you can build a career that feels meaningful and fulfilling.

Identifying Your Passion and Strengths

It's often said that if you love what you do, you'll never work a day in your life. But finding that "thing" you love—your passion—can be much trickier than it sounds. We live in a world full of options and opinions, where it's easy to get lost in what everyone else is doing. But your career path should be about what *you* are drawn to, not what others expect you to do.

The key to identifying your passion lies in self-awareness. What excites you? What activities make you lose track of time? What skills come naturally to you, the ones that feel effortless? Often, our true strengths and passions aren't obvious at first glance; they're woven into the experiences and moments we feel most engaged. You may find passion in solving complex problems, creating something from scratch, helping others grow, or leading a team toward a shared goal.

Take time to reflect on the things that spark joy or curiosity in you. Ask yourself questions like:

- What do I naturally gravitate toward, even when it's not part of my job?

- What activities make me feel most energized and alive?

- When do I feel most confident and capable?

Your passion is likely linked to your innate strengths, and when you align your career with what excites you, it doesn't just become a job—it becomes a calling.

Exercise: Take a moment to jot down your answers to the questions above. Write freely, without judgment or limitation. These answers will serve as a powerful guide as you start to map out your career journey.

Setting the Right Goals from Day One

Once you have a clearer sense of your passion and strengths, it's time to set goals. But not just any goals—*the right* goals. Too often, we're taught to chase after external markers of success: a title, a salary, or recognition. While these can be important, they shouldn't be the sole measure of your career success. Your goals should align with your values and long-term vision for both your career and your life.

Start with the big picture: Where do you want to be in five, ten, or twenty years? It's okay if you don't have every detail figured out yet. The important thing is to have a direction. Once you have a rough idea of your long-term vision, break it down into smaller, achievable milestones. These smaller goals will act as stepping stones that keep you on track, motivated, and moving forward.

Remember, setting the right goals isn't just about ambition; it's about clarity and intention. Ask yourself:

- What impact do I want to have through my work?

- How can my strengths contribute to the greater good?

- What are the non-negotiables in my career and life?

As you work toward your goals, keep them flexible. Life and work can be unpredictable, and sometimes, the best opportunities show up in unexpected ways. But always stay anchored to your values and your long-term vision.

Exercise: Write down your long-term career vision and break it down into three major goals for the next year, three years, and five years. Make sure these goals reflect not only your ambitions but also the lifestyle you envision for yourself.

The Power of Persistence: Why Giving Up Isn't an Option

The path to a successful career is rarely linear. You'll face setbacks, roadblocks, and moments of doubt. It's easy to feel defeated when things don't go as planned or when you hit a wall. But one of the most powerful traits you can cultivate is *persistence*.

Persistence isn't about ignoring your limitations or pretending everything is fine when it's not. It's about staying committed to your goals even when the journey feels tough. It's understanding that failure is a part of success, and each setback is simply a lesson in disguise. Every successful person, from entrepreneurs to artists to CEOs, has faced failure. What sets them apart isn't their avoidance of failure—it's their ability to keep going after they've failed.

Think of your career as a marathon, not a sprint. It's the consistent, small efforts that add up over time. Whether you're learning a new skill, making a tough decision, or navigating a difficult project, persistence will keep you going when motivation fades. The difference between those who succeed and those who don't often comes down to one simple thing: the willingness to keep showing up.

Remember, it's okay to take breaks, reevaluate your path, and even pivot when necessary. But never confuse a temporary setback with permanent defeat. The most important thing is to keep moving forward, even when it's hard.

Exercise: Reflect on a time when you faced a challenge and persisted through it. What did you learn? How did that experience shape who you are today? Write it down, and let it serve as a reminder that persistence is your ally.

Building a great career is like laying the foundation of a house—it takes time, patience, and hard work. But with the right focus, the right goals, and the perseverance to stay the course, you can create something strong, lasting, and uniquely yours. In the next chapter, we'll dive deeper into how to build your professional identity and make your mark in the world.

Chapter Two

Building Your Professional Identity

Your professional identity is more than just your job title or your resume—it's the way you present yourself, the way others perceive you, and the value you bring to your work and your industry. In today's competitive job market, building a strong professional identity is essential not just for career success, but for finding fulfillment in the work you do. This chapter will help you craft your personal brand, leverage your network, and stand out in a sea of applicants.

Crafting Your Personal Brand

Personal branding is one of the most powerful tools you can use to carve out your place in the professional world. It's how you present yourself—what you stand for, what you're known for, and how you communicate your value to others. While it might sound like a buzzword, your personal brand is crucial for building credibility, establishing trust, and making an impact in your industry.

But how do you craft your brand? It begins with introspection. To understand your personal brand, you need to first understand *who you are*. Here are some key questions to guide you:

- **What makes you unique?** What sets you apart from others in your field? Is it your problem-solving ability, your creativity, your leadership skills, or something else?

- **What values do you stand for?** Do you prioritize integrity, innovation, collaboration, or something else in your work? Let your values shape how you present yourself.

- **What's your story?** How did you get to where you are today? Sharing your journey—whether it's full of twists, turns, or straight lines—helps people connect with you on a deeper level.

- **How do you want to be remembered?** Think long-term: When people think of you, what do you want them to remember? What impression do you want to leave behind?

Once you have answers to these questions, you can begin crafting your personal brand. It should come through in your professional presence—whether that's through the way you communicate online, the projects you take on, or the way you interact with others. This consistency will help reinforce your identity and make you memorable.

Exercise: Write a brief "elevator pitch" about yourself. This should be a 30-second summary that conveys what you do, what makes you unique, and what you stand for. Practice delivering it until it feels natural. This will help you introduce yourself in any networking situation or job interview.

Leveraging Networks for Career Growth

You've probably heard the saying, "It's not what you know, but who you know." While this can be somewhat of an oversimplification, there's truth to it: networking can open doors to opportunities that you might not have access to otherwise. But networking isn't just about collecting business cards or adding connections on LinkedIn. It's about building meaningful relationships that can help both you and others grow professionally.

The key to leveraging your network is not to approach it with a transactional mindset—networking isn't about asking for favors, but about giving and sharing. When you approach networking with the goal of genuinely connecting, offering value, and being of help, you'll naturally find that your own career grows as well.

Start by identifying who's in your network. Your current colleagues, former classmates, mentors, and even acquaintances can all be valuable connections. Here are a few strategies for building and leveraging your network:

- **Invest time in building relationships.** Networking doesn't happen overnight. Take the time to build trust and rapport with people. Follow up after meetings, show interest in their work, and offer help when you can.

- **Be authentic.** People can sense when you're being insincere, so don't try to force connections. Be yourself, share your true interests, and engage in conversations that are meaningful.

- **Give before you ask.** Whether it's offering advice, sharing an article, or introducing someone to a helpful connection, always think about how you can provide value first. This builds goodwill and strengthens relationships over time.

- **Stay active online.** In today's digital age, social media platforms like LinkedIn are essential for staying visible and connecting with others in your field. Regularly post insights, comment on others' posts, and share professional achievements or challenges.

Networking is a long-term investment. As your network grows, so too do the opportunities for career advancement. Remember, it's not just about *who* you know, but *how* you engage with them that matters.

Exercise: Take a few minutes to identify three people you'd like to reconnect with or reach out to. Craft a thoughtful message—whether it's to catch up, share an interesting article, or offer help—and send it. This simple action can reignite important connections in your network.

How to Stand Out in a Crowded Job Market

In today's competitive job market, it can feel like everyone is vying for the same opportunities. So, how do you stand out from the crowd? How do you go from being one of many applicants to the person they can't wait to hire? It starts with showcasing your unique value proposition—what you bring to the table that others don't.

To stand out, consider the following strategies:

- **Highlight your unique skills and experiences.** What's something you can do that few others can? It could be a combination of technical expertise, creative problem-solving, leadership experience, or a niche skill set. Emphasize these in your resume, cover letters, and interviews.

- **Tailor your approach.** Whether it's your resume, LinkedIn profile, or the way you apply for jobs, tailor each application to the specific role and company. Highlight your relevant experience, skills, and why you're a perfect fit for their unique needs.

Generic applications won't set you apart; specificity will.

- **Demonstrate results, not just responsibilities.** Employers want to know what you've accomplished, not just what you've done. When describing your work experience, focus on outcomes. Did you increase sales? Improve efficiency? Solve a critical problem? These results show your true impact.

- **Get involved in your industry.** Be more than just a passive observer. Attend industry events, join professional groups, and contribute to conversations in your field. When you engage with others in your industry, you build visibility and credibility—both of which can help you stand out.

- **Keep learning.** Continuous learning is essential in today's fast-moving world. Stay on top of new trends, technologies, and methodologies in your field. Whether through formal education, online courses, or self-directed learning, staying current shows potential employers that you're committed to growth.

The key to standing out is understanding that you don't need to be everything to everyone. Focus on what makes you exceptional, and put that front and center. When you're authentic, clear on your value, and proactive in your career, it's much easier to make a lasting impression.

Exercise: Take a look at your resume, LinkedIn profile, or personal website. Is there a clear distinction of what makes you unique? If not, revise one section to emphasize your standout skills, achievements, or experiences. This can help you create a compelling, memorable professional identity.

Building your professional identity is not about becoming someone you're not—it's about refining who you already are and amplifying the value you bring. By crafting your personal brand, leveraging your network, and standing out in a crowded market, you can set yourself apart and position yourself for long-term success. In the next chapter, we'll explore how to navigate career transitions and continue building on your foundation.

Chapter Three

Navigating Career Transitions

Career transitions are inevitable. Whether you're shifting roles, changing industries, or responding to setbacks, how you navigate these transitions can make all the difference in your professional growth. Transitions often come with uncertainty, fear, and doubt, but they also bring opportunities for reinvention and renewal. This chapter will guide you through how to make big career moves, turn setbacks into opportunities, and embrace uncertainty to build resilience in your professional journey.

Making Big Moves: When to Change Paths

Sometimes, you reach a point in your career where you realize that the path you're on no longer aligns with your goals or passions. You may feel restless, unfulfilled, or simply ready for something new. It's at this crossroads that the decision to make a big move—whether that means switching industries, roles, or even careers—becomes essential. But how do you know when it's time for a change?

Here are a few signs that it may be time to make a move:

- **You're no longer challenged.** When you've mastered your current job and find that you're no longer excited about your work, it could be a sign that you've outgrown your current role. Seeking new challenges or learning opportunities can reignite your passion and drive.

- **You're unhappy.** While all jobs have their ups and downs, a constant feeling of dissatisfaction or unhappiness could mean that something deeper is at play. If your job is draining your energy and doesn't align with your values, it may be time to explore new opportunities that better suit you.

- **You've gained new skills or interests.** As you evolve professionally, you may discover new interests or develop new skills that open doors to different career paths. If you've been cultivating expertise in an area outside your current role, it might be time to make a move in that direction.

- **You're feeling burnt out.** If the thought of your workday fills you with dread, and you find yourself consistently exhausted or disengaged, burnout could be a sign that you need to reassess your career. A change in direction could provide the mental and emotional reset you need.

Making a big career move doesn't always mean a complete 180. Sometimes, it's simply a matter of pivoting—finding a way to apply your skills in a new environment, role, or industry. But it does require courage, self-reflection, and a willingness to embrace the unknown.

Exercise: Take a moment to reflect on your current job. Are you feeling stagnant, uninspired, or burnt out? If so, list three potential directions you might consider moving toward. These could be new industries, roles, or ways to expand your current skillset. Don't limit yourself—let your imagination flow freely.

Turning Setbacks into Stepping Stones

Setbacks are an unavoidable part of any career journey. Whether it's a failed project, a missed promotion, or a job loss, setbacks can feel like a blow to your confidence and momentum. However, it's important to remember that setbacks are not the end—they can be the beginning of something greater.

How you respond to setbacks often defines your success. Instead of letting a setback discourage you, try to view it as an opportunity for growth and learning. Here's how:

- **Reframe your mindset.** Instead of seeing a setback as a failure, view it as a lesson. What can you learn from the situation? What went wrong, and how can you prevent it from happening again? This mindset shift turns setbacks into valuable learning experiences.

- **Take responsibility without self-blame.** It's easy to fall into the trap of blaming yourself when things don't go as planned. However, acknowledging your role in the situation (without being overly harsh on yourself) allows you to take control of your future actions and decisions.

- **Stay resilient.** Resilience isn't about bouncing back immediately; it's about building the strength to continue moving forward, even when things don't go your way. It's about having the patience to regroup, reevaluate, and take action again.

- **Celebrate small victories.** Sometimes, setbacks can make you feel like you're stuck in a rut. Celebrate the small wins—whether it's landing a new interview, completing a challenging task, or making progress on your next big project. These little victories can help you stay motivated and keep moving forward.

Remember, setbacks are often just detours on the way to something greater. Many successful people have faced significant setbacks before achieving their goals. What matters is how you handle them and use them to fuel your growth.

Exercise: Think of a recent setback or challenge you've faced in your career. Write down what you learned from the experience. How did it help you grow? What changes will you make to ensure you're better prepared for similar challenges in the future?

Embracing Uncertainty and Building Resilience

Uncertainty is one of the constants of a career. Whether it's a market shift, organizational changes, or unexpected challenges, uncertainty can feel overwhelming. However, learning to embrace uncertainty—and building resilience—can transform fear into a powerful tool for growth.

Resilience is the ability to adapt, bounce back from adversity, and keep going despite the obstacles in your way. It's about accepting that things won't always go as planned, but choosing to keep moving forward anyway.

Here's how to build resilience in your career:

- **Develop a growth mindset.** People with a growth mindset view challenges as opportunities to learn and grow, rather than as threats. Embrace the idea that every setback or obstacle is an opportunity to improve your skills and become better equipped for future challenges.

- **Cultivate self-compassion.** Resilience doesn't mean pushing yourself to the breaking point. Be kind to yourself when things don't go well. Take time to recover, recharge, and reflect on what you've learned. Self-compassion gives you the strength to keep moving forward, even when things aren't going perfectly.

- **Stay flexible.** Career paths are rarely linear. Being open to change and new opportunities can help you navigate the uncertainties of the job market and make the most of unexpected turns in your career.

- **Find support.** Resilience is not about going it alone. Surround yourself with a strong support system—whether it's friends, family, mentors, or colleagues. Having people who believe in you and offer guidance and encouragement can help you navigate even the toughest challenges.

Embracing uncertainty means trusting yourself to adapt and thrive, no matter what comes your way. The more you practice resilience, the more confident you'll feel when facing the unknown.

Exercise: Reflect on a time when you faced uncertainty in your career. How did you handle it? What did you learn from the experience? Write down three actions you can take next time you encounter uncertainty to strengthen your resilience.

Career transitions are never easy, but they're an integral part of your professional growth. Whether you're making a big move, turning a setback into a stepping stone, or embracing the uncertainty of the future, remember that each transition holds an opportunity to redefine your career and build a life that aligns with your values and goals. In the next chapter, we'll explore how to sustain your success and continue growing professionally over the long term.

Chapter Four

Skills for Success

Success isn't just about working hard—it's about working smart. And to work smart, you need to develop and refine a set of skills that not only help you perform well in your current job but also position you for growth and advancement throughout your career. In this chapter, we'll explore the essential skills for career advancement, the importance of lifelong learning, and how to hone your communication and leadership abilities. These skills will become the foundation for your continued professional success.

Essential Skills for Career Advancement

To move ahead in your career, there are certain foundational skills that can't be overlooked. While technical expertise in your field is critical, soft skills—such as problem-solving, adaptability, and emotional intelligence—are just as essential. These are the skills that will allow you to thrive in a fast-changing work environment, build strong relationships, and demonstrate the leadership potential that employers value.

Here are some key skills to focus on:

- **Problem-Solving:** The ability to identify challenges, analyze situations, and come up with creative solutions is invaluable. Employers are constantly looking for individuals who can think critically and find ways to overcome obstacles.

- **Time Management:** Success often comes down to being able to manage your time effectively. Prioritize your tasks, stay organized, and avoid procrastination. Efficient time management helps you meet deadlines and shows that you're reliable and focused.

- **Adaptability:** The workplace is constantly evolving, and being adaptable means you're ready for whatever changes come your way. Whether it's adjusting to new technology, a change in team dynamics, or an unexpected shift in responsibilities, adaptability shows that you can thrive no matter the circumstances.

- **Collaboration and Teamwork:** No one achieves success alone. The ability to work well with others, listen, and contribute meaningfully to a team is essential. Whether you're in a leadership position or part of a team, collaboration helps everyone move forward together.

- **Emotional Intelligence:** The ability to understand and manage your own emotions, as well as recognize and influence the emotions of others, is crucial for building strong relationships. High emotional intelligence fosters better communication, conflict resolution, and overall teamwork.

Lifelong Learning: Always Be Growing

In today's rapidly changing job market, what you know today may not be sufficient tomorrow. Lifelong learning is no longer a luxury—it's a necessity. Continuously updating your skills and knowledge not only helps you stay competitive but also keeps you engaged and motivated in your work.

Lifelong learning doesn't have to mean going back to school or getting another degree. It can be as simple as:

- **Reading industry-related books, articles, and blogs.** Stay informed about the latest trends and developments in your field by regularly reading material that expands your knowledge.

- **Taking online courses or certifications.** Many platforms offer affordable or free courses in a variety of fields. These can range from technical skills (like programming or data analysis) to soft skills (like communication or leadership).

- **Seeking feedback and mentorship.** Learning from others is an invaluable resource. Find mentors who can guide you through your career, and seek feedback to understand your strengths and areas for growth.

- **Attending workshops and seminars.** Whether in person or online, workshops and seminars offer opportunities to expand your skillset and connect with others in your industry.

Remember, learning isn't confined to a classroom. Every experience—whether it's a new project at work, a challenging conversation, or a failure—offers lessons that contribute to your growth.

Exercise: Identify one skill you'd like to improve. It could be something technical (like learning a new software) or a soft skill (like improving your public speaking). Research resources (books, online courses, or mentors) that can help you improve in that area, and commit to taking one step toward learning something new in the next week.

How to Hone Your Communication and Leadership Abilities

Communication and leadership are two of the most powerful tools in your career toolbox. These skills not only help you express your ideas clearly and effectively but also position you as someone capable of leading others toward a shared vision. Whether you're aiming for a leadership role or simply want to improve how you engage with others, honing these abilities will set you apart.

- **Communication Skills:** Effective communication is more than just speaking clearly—it's about ensuring that your message is heard, understood, and acted upon. Strong communicators are good listeners, ask thoughtful questions, and adapt their message to their audience. Here are a few tips for improving your communication:

- **Active listening:** Pay full attention when others are speaking and show that you're engaged by nodding or paraphrasing what they've said. Listening actively helps build trust and makes your responses more relevant.

- **Clarity and conciseness:** Be clear and to the point. Avoid jargon or overly complex language that could confuse your audience. The goal is to make sure your message is easily understood.

- **Non-verbal communication:** Your body language, tone of voice, and facial expressions play a huge role in how your message is received. Make sure your non-verbal cues align with your words.

- **Confidence:** Confidence in communication comes from knowing your subject matter and having a clear message. Practice speaking confidently and comfortably, even if it's in smaller groups before addressing larger audiences.

- **Leadership Skills:** Leadership isn't just about managing people—it's about inspiring them, guiding them, and helping them achieve their potential. Whether you're managing a team or leading by influence, these tips will help you develop as a leader:

  - **Lead by example:** The best leaders set the tone by modeling the behavior and values they want to see in others. Your actions should align with your words, showing integrity, responsibility, and respect.

  - **Empathy and support:** Good leaders understand the needs, concerns, and motivations of those they lead. Offer support, provide feedback, and help others grow both personally and professionally.

- ○ **Vision and inspiration:** A great leader has a clear vision of where they want to go and can inspire others to follow that path. Share your vision with your team and make it compelling so others are excited to be part of the journey.

- ○ **Decisiveness:** Leaders must make decisions, sometimes under pressure. Being able to make tough calls, while considering the long-term consequences, is essential for effective leadership.

Exercise: Identify someone who you admire as a communicator or leader. What qualities do they exhibit that you'd like to develop in yourself? Write down one thing you can do this week to improve your communication or leadership abilities. It could be something small, like speaking up in a meeting or offering support to a colleague.

Success in your career requires a blend of skills—technical abilities, soft skills, and personal development. By cultivating essential skills like problem-solving, time management, adaptability, and emotional intelligence, you can set yourself up for career growth. Combine that with a commitment to lifelong learning and a focus on honing your communication and leadership abilities, and you'll be well on your way to achieving your career goals. In the next chapter, we'll explore how to sustain success and continue growing in the long run.

Chapter Five

Creating Meaningful Relationships

Success in any career isn't just about what you know—it's about who you know and, more importantly, how you build and maintain meaningful relationships. This chapter focuses on the power of networking with intention and integrity, the role of mentors in your journey, and how to build genuine, supportive connections that will not only help you grow professionally but enrich your personal life as well.

Networking with Intention and Integrity

Networking often gets a bad reputation. It's sometimes seen as a transactional activity—a way to collect business cards or

LinkedIn connections without real relationships forming. But true networking is so much more. It's about building authentic connections with people who share common values, goals, or interests, and helping one another along the way.

To network effectively, you need to approach it with intention and integrity. Here are a few tips for making your networking efforts meaningful:

- **Be Genuine:** Networking isn't about getting something from others—it's about creating mutually beneficial relationships. Approach each interaction with curiosity and a desire to understand the other person's goals, challenges, and experiences. When you build connections based on genuine interest, they will be far more impactful than ones based purely on self-interest.

- **Focus on Quality, Not Quantity:** Rather than trying to connect with as many people as possible, focus on building deeper relationships with a select group of individuals who align with your values or can support you in your career growth. Strong, lasting relationships are more valuable than a long list of contacts.

- **Give Before You Get:** The best way to build meaningful connections is to offer something before you ask for something in return. Whether it's sharing helpful resources, providing introductions, or offering your expertise, people will appreciate your generosity and be more inclined to reciprocate.

- **Consistency is Key:** Networking is not a one-time event—it's an ongoing process. Attend events, follow up after meetings, and stay in touch with your connections. Send a quick email to check in or share something you think might interest them. Relationships are built over time, not in one conversation.

Exercise: Identify three people you've recently met or connected with professionally. Reach out to each of them with a thoughtful message that focuses on their needs or interests, not your own. How can you help them today?

Finding Mentors and Becoming One

Mentorship is a powerful tool for growth, both for the mentee and the mentor. A mentor can offer guidance, share valuable experiences, and help you navigate your career challenges. But mentoring isn't just about receiving advice—it's about developing a relationship built on trust, respect, and mutual growth. The best mentorships evolve into long-term, impactful relationships that benefit both parties.

Finding a Mentor:

- **Look for Experience and Wisdom:** Your mentor doesn't have to be in the exact same field as you, but they should have experience that can guide you. Look for someone who has faced challenges, taken risks, and achieved success in their career. This person doesn't have to be at the very top of their field but should possess a level of experience you admire.

- **Seek Out Leaders You Respect:** A mentor is someone who leads with integrity, empathy, and insight. Seek individuals who have values aligned with yours and who have a reputation for helping others grow. These leaders often have invaluable lessons to share that go beyond technical skills.

- **Be Clear About What You Need:** Mentorship is most effective when both parties understand what they expect from the relationship. Be clear about what you hope to gain from the mentorship. Are you seeking guidance on career choices, work-life balance, leadership skills, or something else? This clarity will help your mentor know how they can best support you.

Becoming a Mentor:

- **Share Your Knowledge:** If you've had success in your career, you likely have insights, strategies, and experiences that could help someone else. Be open to sharing these lessons with those who are just starting their careers or looking for guidance.

- **Be Supportive, Not Directive:** A good mentor doesn't just tell their mentee what to do. They guide, encourage, and help the mentee discover their own path. Instead of giving specific solutions, ask questions that encourage reflection and critical thinking.

- **Invest in the Relationship:** Mentorship is a two-way street. It requires time, attention, and care from both the mentor and mentee. Be present in the relationship and show a genuine interest in the other person's growth. The impact you have as a mentor will resonate long after the formal relationship ends.

Exercise: Identify someone in your life who could benefit from your knowledge and experience. Reach out to offer mentorship or guidance. Even a short conversation could be incredibly valuable to someone just starting their journey.

Building Genuine, Supportive Connections at Work and Beyond

At work, relationships with colleagues, clients, and managers shape your daily experience. Building strong, supportive relationships within your professional network can make your work life more rewarding and help you navigate challenges with a sense of camaraderie. Beyond the office, personal relationships also play a huge role in overall success, offering support, perspective, and balance.

Fostering Relationships at Work:

- **Be Approachable and Collaborative:** A supportive work environment is one where colleagues feel comfortable sharing ideas, feedback, and challenges. Be the kind of person who listens actively, values others' input, and offers constructive support. This fosters a collaborative and positive culture that can help everyone excel.

- **Show Appreciation:** Small gestures of appreciation can go a long way in strengthening professional relationships. Recognize others' hard work, share credit for achievements, and celebrate wins together. Gratitude fosters a culture of mutual respect and trust.

- **Handle Conflicts with Integrity:** Conflict is inevitable in any workplace, but it doesn't have to be destructive. Approach conflicts with a mindset of collaboration and resolution, rather than confrontation. Respectfully addressing disagreements and working toward solutions will strengthen relationships and your reputation as a team player.

Building Connections Outside of Work:

- **Invest in Personal Relationships:** Building relationships outside of work provides balance and a support system that's crucial for your well-being. Whether it's friends, family, or a community group, nurturing these connections helps you stay grounded, motivated, and resilient when facing challenges.

- **Be a Connector:** Help others make connections by introducing people who could benefit from knowing each other. Being a connector not only strengthens your relationships but also solidifies your reputation as someone who adds value to others' lives.

- **Support Others' Goals:** Helping others achieve their personal and professional goals not only strengthens your bond but also creates a positive ripple effect. When you support others, they are more likely to support you in return, leading to mutually beneficial relationships.

Exercise: Identify one relationship—either at work or in your personal life—that you would like to strengthen. Take one action this week to deepen that connection, whether it's offering support, checking in, or simply spending more time together.

In summary, creating meaningful relationships takes time, effort, and authenticity. Networking with intention, finding and becoming a mentor, and building supportive connections both at work and beyond will create a strong network that nurtures your personal and professional growth. These relationships will help you navigate the highs and lows of your career and enrich your life in ways you might not expect.

Chapter Six

Work-Life Balance

In today's fast-paced, always-connected world, finding work-life balance is more important—and more challenging—than ever. Success in your career doesn't have to come at the expense of your health, relationships, or personal happiness. This chapter explores how to set boundaries, prioritize well-being, manage your time efficiently, and avoid burnout, so you can lead a fulfilling life both at work and at home.

Setting Boundaries and Prioritizing Well-being

In a culture that often values hustle and nonstop productivity, setting clear boundaries between work and personal life can feel daunting. But without boundaries, you risk burnout, stress, and a sense of losing control over your time. Healthy boundaries are essential for ensuring that you can be present both at work and in your personal life, without sacrificing one for the other.

Setting Boundaries:

- **Define Your Limits:** Take time to reflect on what matters most to you, both in your career and in your personal life. What are your non-negotiables? Whether it's time with family, exercise, or a hobby, knowing your limits will help you set boundaries that protect your time and energy.

- **Communicate Clearly:** Boundaries are only effective when they're communicated openly. Whether it's setting work hours, taking breaks, or reserving time for personal activities, be clear with your colleagues, managers, and family members about what you need. A simple "I'm unavailable after 6 p.m." or "I need my weekends for personal time" can help create a clear line between work and life.

- **Respect Your Own Boundaries:** It's easy to set boundaries but difficult to enforce them, especially when work demands pull you in. Remind yourself regularly that prioritizing your well-being is not only important for you but also for the quality of your work and relationships. Practice self-respect by honoring the boundaries you've set.

Prioritizing Well-being:

- **Self-Care Isn't Selfish:** Prioritizing your health, mental well-being, and happiness is essential for maintaining long-term success. Take care of your physical and mental health with regular exercise, sufficient sleep, healthy eating, and time for relaxation. Taking care of yourself doesn't just improve your personal life—it also enhances your professional performance.

- **Mental Health Matters:** It's easy to neglect your mental well-being in the pursuit of success, but stress, anxiety, and exhaustion can seriously impair your ability to perform at your best. Build habits to protect your mental health, such as mindfulness, meditation, journaling, or therapy. These practices allow you to recharge and stay grounded during challenging times.

Exercise: Take a moment to list your personal non-negotiables. What are the activities or relationships that are essential to your well-being? Now, identify one boundary you could implement in the next week to protect those priorities.

Time Management for a Balanced Life

Effective time management is crucial for achieving work-life balance. With so many responsibilities pulling you in different directions, it can feel impossible to get everything done. But with the right time management strategies, you can accomplish more, reduce stress, and carve out time for what really matters.

Time Management Strategies:

- **Plan Your Week in Advance:** At the start of each week, take time to review your calendar and prioritize your tasks. Identify the most important tasks that align with your long-term goals and tackle those first. Use a planner or digital calendar to keep track of deadlines and commitments.

- **Set Realistic Goals:** While it's important to aim high, setting overly ambitious goals can lead to disappointment and frustration. Break down larger projects into manageable tasks and set achievable daily and weekly goals. This way, you can celebrate small wins along the way, which boosts motivation and keeps you on track.

- **Use Time Blocks:** Time-blocking is a technique where you allocate specific chunks of time to tasks or activities. For example, you might set aside 9 a.m. to 11 a.m. for deep work, 11 a.m. to 12 p.m. for meetings, and 1 p.m. to 3 p.m. for emails. This minimizes distractions and allows you to stay focused on one task at a time.

- **Delegate and Ask for Help:** Time management isn't just about managing your own tasks—it's also about recognizing when you need help. Don't hesitate to delegate tasks at work or ask your partner or family members to share responsibilities at home. Learning to ask for support is a key part of managing your time effectively.

- **Set Boundaries for Technology Use:** Technology can be a huge time-suck if not managed properly. Set boundaries for when and how you check emails, social media, and work-related notifications. Consider using tools like "Do Not Disturb" or time-tracking apps to help you stay focused on what matters.

Exercise: Choose one time management strategy you'll implement this week. Whether it's time-blocking, delegating tasks, or setting weekly goals, commit to following it for the next seven days. At the end of the week, reflect on how it affected your productivity and stress levels.

How to Avoid Burnout and Stay Energized

Burnout is a real and growing concern for professionals across industries. It's easy to push yourself to the brink of exhaustion in pursuit of career success, but doing so can have long-term negative effects on both your physical and mental health. The key to avoiding burnout lies in creating a sustainable routine, staying connected to your purpose, and learning how to recharge when you need it.

Recognizing the Signs of Burnout:

Burnout doesn't happen overnight—it's a gradual process. Early signs of burnout include:

- Feeling physically and emotionally drained even after a break.

- Difficulty finding joy or satisfaction in your work.

- Increased irritability or frustration.

- A sense of being disconnected from your colleagues or purpose.

If you're experiencing these symptoms, it's important to take them seriously and address them before they worsen.

Preventing Burnout:

- **Take Breaks:** In our work-driven culture, it's easy to overlook the importance of breaks. But regularly stepping away from your tasks—whether it's a short walk, a lunch break, or a vacation—helps refresh your mind and body, preventing exhaustion from building up.

- **Practice Work-Life Integration, Not Just Balance:** Instead of compartmentalizing work and life, practice integrating both in a way that suits you. For example, you might schedule some work time during off-hours when you're more focused, or use a flexible work schedule to accommodate personal commitments.

- **Know When to Rest:** Understand that rest is not a luxury; it's a necessity. If you're feeling overwhelmed or tired, it's okay to step back. Prioritize sleep and recovery to ensure you're operating at your best.

- **Find Joy Outside of Work:** Your career is important, but it should never define you entirely. Cultivate hobbies, passions, and relationships outside of work to recharge and maintain a sense of balance. Whether it's traveling, reading, cooking, or spending time with loved ones, make space for activities that bring you joy.

Exercise: Reflect on your current routine and identify areas where you might be overextending yourself. What can you do to create more balance and prevent burnout? Choose one action to take this week to start protecting your energy and well-being.

Work-life balance isn't something you achieve once and then forget about—it's an ongoing process of self-awareness, boundary-setting, and intentional living. By setting clear boundaries, managing your time wisely, and taking steps to prevent burnout, you can create a balanced life that allows you to thrive both personally and professionally.

Chapter Seven

Navigating Challenges with Confidence

No matter how successful we become, challenges are a natural part of the journey. What separates those who rise from those who falter is not the absence of obstacles but the way they face them. This chapter will explore how to turn obstacles into opportunities, master self-advocacy, and deal with criticism constructively. By developing the skills to navigate challenges confidently, you'll build resilience, grow from setbacks, and emerge stronger than ever.

Turning Obstacles into Opportunities

Obstacles are often seen as roadblocks, barriers to success, or things that stand in the way of our goals. But the most successful people know that obstacles aren't the end—they are just detours that can lead to unexpected opportunities.

Reframe Your Mindset:

The first step in turning obstacles into opportunities is shifting your perspective. Instead of seeing setbacks as failures, view them as challenges to learn from. Ask yourself questions like:

- What is this situation teaching me?

- How can I use this experience to grow?

- What new skills or insights can I gain from this obstacle?

A positive mindset helps you stay focused on solutions rather than problems. When you look at an obstacle as an opportunity to innovate, you begin to see possibilities where others might see limitations.

Example: If you're facing a challenging project at work, instead of feeling defeated, view it as a chance to learn new skills or demonstrate your problem-solving abilities. The lessons learned from overcoming difficulties often become the foundations of future success.

Practice Resilience:

Resilience is the ability to bounce back after adversity, and it is one of the most important qualities to cultivate when navigating challenges. While setbacks are inevitable, resilience helps you stay grounded and move forward.

- **Stay Composed:** When obstacles arise, it's easy to become overwhelmed. However, keeping a level head allows you to approach challenges more clearly and with a sense of control.

- **Learn from Failure:** The most successful people are those who have failed the most. Every failure is a stepping stone to eventual success. Learn from each experience, and you will continue to grow stronger and more capable.

Exercise: Think of an obstacle you've faced recently. How did you reframe it as an opportunity? Write down the lessons you've learned from overcoming this challenge. What strengths did it reveal in you?

Mastering Self-Advocacy and Confidence

Self-advocacy is the ability to speak up for yourself, assert your needs, and advocate for your value in the workplace and in your personal life. It's not about being pushy or arrogant—it's about recognizing your worth and expressing it confidently.

Understanding Your Value:

To advocate for yourself effectively, you first need to understand your value. This involves knowing your strengths, accomplishments, and what you bring to the table. Confidence doesn't come from pretending to be something you're not; it comes from a deep understanding of who you are and what you contribute.

- **Know Your Strengths:** Take time to reflect on your unique skills and attributes. Write them down. What do others come to you for help with? What accomplishments are you most proud of?

- **Celebrate Your Achievements:** Confidence is built on a history of success, no matter how small the wins may seem. Take pride in your progress and the steps you've taken toward achieving your goals.

Effective Self-Advocacy:

- **Speak Up:** When you have ideas or feedback, don't be afraid to share them. Whether it's asking for a raise, pitching a new idea, or voicing your opinion in a meeting, speaking up demonstrates your confidence and your commitment to contributing.

- **Ask for What You Need:** If you need resources, support, or recognition, don't wait for someone to offer it. Be proactive in asking for what will help you succeed.

- **Negotiate with Confidence:** Negotiating isn't just about salary—it's about securing the resources, time, and space you need to thrive in your role. Approach negotiation with the mindset of a partnership rather than a confrontation.

Example: If you're seeking a promotion, instead of waiting for it to come to you, initiate the conversation. Highlight your achievements, demonstrate your value, and express your desire for more responsibility. When done with confidence and clarity, self-advocacy can open doors to new opportunities.

Exercise: Write a list of your top three achievements in the last six months. How can you use these accomplishments to advocate for yourself in future career discussions, whether in performance reviews or networking?

Dealing with Criticism and Finding Constructive Feedback

Criticism can be tough to hear, especially when it feels personal. However, feedback—whether positive or negative—can be one of your greatest tools for growth. The key is learning how to respond to criticism in a way that strengthens your skills and builds your confidence.

Reframe Criticism as a Learning Opportunity:

Instead of viewing criticism as a negative reflection of your abilities, reframe it as a valuable resource for improvement. Ask yourself:

- What can I learn from this feedback?

- How can I apply this constructive criticism to improve?

- Is there an underlying truth in this feedback that I can work on?

When you shift your mindset from defensiveness to curiosity, criticism becomes less about your personal shortcomings and more about your potential for growth.

Seek Constructive Feedback:

Don't wait for feedback to come to you—actively seek it out. Regularly asking for feedback shows that you're committed to self-improvement and are open to learning. Whether it's from a supervisor, a mentor, or peers, feedback provides insight into areas you might not see yourself.

- **Be Specific:** When requesting feedback, ask for specific areas of improvement. Instead of asking, "How am I doing?" try asking, "What is one thing I could do better in my role?" This invites actionable, focused feedback.

- **Act on Feedback:** Receiving feedback is only valuable if you take steps to act on it. After receiving feedback, create an action plan to address the areas that need improvement. This shows that you're committed to continuous development.

Handling Negative Feedback Gracefully:

- **Don't Take It Personally:** Negative feedback isn't about you as a person—it's about your performance. Keep a level head and focus on the facts of the situation.

- **Acknowledge and Thank:** Even if the feedback stings, thank the person giving it. It takes courage to give constructive criticism, and acknowledging it respectfully demonstrates professionalism and maturity.

Example: If a manager tells you that your reports are lacking in detail, don't feel discouraged. Instead, ask for clarification on which areas need improvement, and then take steps to address those weaknesses. Over time, this makes you a stronger, more capable professional.

Exercise: Reflect on a piece of criticism you've received recently. How did you initially react? Now, write down how you could reframe it as an opportunity for growth. What specific actions can you take to improve based on this feedback?

The ability to navigate challenges with confidence is a vital skill that will serve you throughout your career and personal life. By viewing obstacles as opportunities, mastering the art of self-advocacy, and handling criticism constructively, you'll continue to grow and develop into a resilient, self-assured professional. Remember, challenges aren't the end—they are part of the process of becoming the best version of yourself. With the right mindset and strategies, you can face any challenge with confidence and emerge stronger than before.

Chapter Eight

Creating a Legacy

Success isn't just about what you accomplish in your own life—it's also about how you impact the lives of others. Creating a meaningful legacy is one of the most fulfilling ways to live, and it doesn't have to come at the end of your career. It starts now. In this chapter, we'll explore how to use your success to lift others, why giving back should be an integral part of your journey, and how living with purpose beyond your career creates a legacy that lasts far beyond your professional achievements.

Using Your Success to Lift Others

As you progress in your career and reach new heights of success, it's easy to become focused solely on your personal achievements. However, true fulfillment often comes from lifting others up along the way. Sharing your success with others and using your position to empower those around you is one of the most powerful ways to create lasting impact.

Mentorship: Guiding the Next Generation

One of the most effective ways to use your success to help others is by becoming a mentor. Mentorship allows you to share your knowledge, experiences, and insights with those who are just starting out or are facing similar challenges you once faced.

- **Invest in Others:** Mentorship doesn't always mean formal coaching or being in a high position of authority. It can be as simple as offering advice, sharing resources, or providing a listening ear when someone needs guidance.

- **Pay It Forward:** The best mentors don't just give advice—they actively create opportunities for others to succeed. By recommending someone for a position, advocating for their ideas, or introducing them to influential contacts, you can play a pivotal role in helping them achieve their goals.

Example: If you've been successful in your field, consider how you might give back through mentorship programs, both formally and informally. Even if you only mentor one person, the impact can be profound.

Empower Others Through Your Influence:

As you move forward in your career, you gain influence. That influence is a powerful tool, and when used for good, it can help raise others up. Whether it's using your platform to highlight issues that matter, advocating for diversity and inclusion, or making a difference in your community, your success becomes a stepping stone for those who are looking up to you.

- **Champion Causes You Believe In:** Whether it's fighting for workplace equality, advocating for education reform, or supporting environmental sustainability, use your influence to amplify voices that might otherwise go unheard.

- **Lead by Example:** People will be more inspired by your actions than your words. Live with integrity, kindness, and a commitment to fairness, and others will be encouraged to follow suit.

Exercise: Reflect on someone who mentored or inspired you along your journey. How can you give back in a similar way to others in your life? What steps can you take to empower the next generation?

Why Giving Back Should Be Part of Your Plan

When you've achieved success, it's easy to become consumed with the need to maintain or grow that success. However, giving back—whether in terms of time, resources, or expertise—shouldn't be an afterthought. It's part of what makes success truly meaningful. Giving back is not just about charity—it's about contributing to the greater good and leaving a positive mark on the world.

The Ripple Effect of Giving:

Giving back can create a ripple effect, inspiring others to do the same. Whether it's donating your time to a cause, funding scholarships for underprivileged students, or starting a charitable organization, each act of kindness and generosity has the power to multiply.

- **Inspire Others to Give:** When you give back, you set an example for those around you. The people you help, the organizations you support, and the causes you champion will encourage others to do the same.

- **Create a Culture of Giving:** In a workplace, community, or personal life, fostering a culture of generosity can lead to collective change. When people see others giving, whether it's with their time, skills, or money, it encourages a sense of shared responsibility and collaboration.

Giving Back Is More Than Money:

While financial contributions are valuable, there are many other ways to give back. Your skills, knowledge, and experience are invaluable resources. Volunteer your time, teach a class, or offer pro bono work to organizations that align with your values. The impact of these contributions can often be just as significant as a monetary donation.

Example: Bill Gates, through the Bill & Melinda Gates Foundation, has donated billions to improve global health and reduce poverty. However, his success didn't just lead him to donate money—it drove him to advocate for policy changes, raise awareness, and inspire other leaders to join the cause. You don't need to be a billionaire to make a difference—you just need to find a cause that matters to you and start taking action.

Exercise: Think of one cause or organization you feel passionate about. How can you contribute your time, skills, or resources to support it? Create a plan for how you can give back in the coming months.

Living with Purpose Beyond the Career

While a fulfilling career is important, it's equally vital to remember that your career is just one aspect of your life. True success lies in living with purpose, in creating a legacy that goes beyond titles, accolades, and paychecks.

Purpose Beyond Professional Success:

Living with purpose means aligning your work and life with your core values. This purpose doesn't have to be tied to your job title. It could be about raising a family, pursuing personal passions, making a difference in your community, or leaving the world a better place.

- **Find Meaning Outside of Work:** While a career can be fulfilling, don't let it define your entire existence. Engage in activities that bring you joy and purpose, whether it's spending time with family, practicing a hobby, or contributing to social causes.

- **Strive for Balance:** A meaningful life is one where career success complements personal fulfillment. Prioritize your well-being, relationships, and passions in addition to your professional achievements. The balance you find will lead to greater happiness and overall life satisfaction.

Creating a Personal Legacy:

The legacy you create is a combination of how you live and the values you instill in others. A legacy isn't necessarily about building something grand—it's about living with integrity, kindness, and purpose. It's about making decisions that are not only good for you but also good for the world around you.

- **Live Authentically:** Be true to yourself. Pursue the things that make you happy, and live according to your values, not the expectations of others.

- **Invest in Relationships:** The relationships you build with family, friends, colleagues, and others are the true treasures of your life. The impact you make on others, the love you share, and the connections you nurture will be your lasting legacy.

Example: Many people look up to public figures like Nelson Mandela, not just for their professional accomplishments but for the way they lived their lives with integrity, compassion, and a commitment to justice. While Mandela's work as a politician and activist was groundbreaking, it was his personal values and character that left a lasting legacy.

Exercise: Think about how you want to be remembered. What values, actions, or contributions do you want to leave behind? Create a vision of your personal legacy and set small, actionable goals to start living it today.

Creating a legacy isn't reserved for the end of your career—it's something that should be cultivated throughout your entire life. By using your success to lift others, prioritizing giving back, and living with purpose beyond your career, you create a legacy that transcends your professional accomplishments. It's about leaving a mark on the world that reflects who you truly are and the difference you made in the lives of others. Remember, the most meaningful legacies are those built on compassion, generosity, and a commitment to creating a better future for those who come after us.

Chapter Nine

The Final Word

As you've worked through the advice and strategies in this book, you've likely encountered moments of clarity, inspiration, and even some self-reflection. This chapter is a reflection on the journey—the one you've already taken and the one that lies ahead. It's about understanding how to keep evolving as a person, both personally and professionally, and how to stay grounded in the goals that have always mattered to you.

The pursuit of a meaningful career and life isn't a one-time effort. It's an ongoing process—one that requires intentional growth, constant self-reflection, and a willingness to adapt as you encounter new challenges and opportunities. Here's how you can continue to evolve while staying true to your core goals.

Reflecting on the Journey

Success isn't defined solely by accomplishments. It's shaped by the lessons learned, the resilience built, and the growth you've experienced along the way. Taking time to reflect on your journey can help you understand how far you've come and clarify what you still want to achieve.

Looking Back to Move Forward:

It's easy to get caught up in the rush of chasing the next big thing, but taking a step back to reflect can offer invaluable insights. Look back on the moments that shaped you—whether they were triumphs, failures, or unexpected twists—and ask yourself:

- What lessons have I learned?

- What decisions had the most impact on my growth?

- How have my values evolved over time?

- What has brought me the most fulfillment?

Celebrate Your Wins, Big and Small:

While it's natural to focus on areas of growth and improvement, don't forget to celebrate the successes you've achieved, both big and small. These milestones are proof of your hard work, persistence, and resilience. Take the time to acknowledge your efforts, whether it's reaching a career goal, overcoming a personal challenge, or simply making progress in a meaningful direction.

- **Practice Gratitude:** Reflect on the people, moments, and experiences that have contributed to your journey. Gratitude fosters contentment and can boost motivation as you move forward.

- **Learn from Mistakes:** Failures are just stepping stones in the path to success. Reflect on the mistakes you've made and think about how they've contributed to your personal growth. The key is not to dwell on them, but to use them as fuel for future success.

Exercise: Set aside time to journal about your journey so far. What have been your proudest moments, and how have you changed as a result? Write down your biggest lessons learned and the areas where you want to continue growing.

How to Keep Evolving and Stay True to Your Goals

The world is constantly changing, and so are you. The key to sustaining long-term success and fulfillment is to keep evolving—to never stop learning, adapting, and growing. But while growth is essential, it's equally important to stay rooted in your values and the goals that have always mattered to you. Here's how to strike that balance.

Continuing Personal Growth:

No matter how much you achieve, personal development should never be a one-time project. Striving for growth is a continuous process, one that requires openness to new experiences, new knowledge, and new ways of thinking. Here's how to keep evolving:

- **Embrace Lifelong Learning:** Keep seeking knowledge and skills that challenge you. Whether it's pursuing formal education, attending conferences, reading books, or learning from your experiences, ongoing education is a cornerstone of personal and professional development.

- **Push Yourself Out of Your Comfort Zone:** Real growth happens when we challenge ourselves. Don't be afraid to take on projects that seem daunting or explore new opportunities that stretch your abilities.

- **Self-Reflection is Key:** Set aside time regularly to assess where you are, where you want to be, and how you're getting there. Self-reflection allows you to recalibrate your actions and remain aligned with your long-term goals.

Staying True to Your Goals:

In the pursuit of success, it's easy to lose sight of why you started. The distractions, the pressure to meet external expectations, and the lure of short-term rewards can all cause you to veer off course. To stay true to your goals, ask yourself these critical questions:

- **Are my actions aligned with my core values?**

- **Am I chasing someone else's dream or my own?**

- **Do I still feel passionate about the goals I set, or is it time to reevaluate them?**

Create a Long-Term Vision:

While day-to-day decisions are important, it's equally important to keep an eye on the bigger picture. Having a long-term vision for your life and career will help you stay focused and make decisions that align with your deeper aspirations.

- **Set Milestones:** Break down your long-term goals into smaller, actionable steps. This allows you to stay on track and celebrate small victories along the way.

- **Review Your Goals Regularly:** Life changes, and so will your goals. Make it a habit to revisit and adjust them as necessary. This ensures that you remain focused on what truly matters to you, not just what seems urgent or trendy.

Example: Oprah Winfrey, despite all of her success, has remained true to her purpose of inspiring and empowering others. She has continually evolved by embracing new challenges (like the launch of OWN) while staying true to her mission of promoting meaningful conversations and personal growth. By aligning her work with her core values, she has created a legacy that transcends her career.

Exercise: Take a moment to write out your long-term vision for your life. Consider where you want to be in 5, 10, or 20 years. What are the core values that you want to guide your journey? How can you break down your goals into manageable steps to ensure steady progress?

The journey to a meaningful career and life is never linear. It's full of twists, turns, and unexpected changes, but with reflection, continuous growth, and a commitment to your true values, you'll continue to evolve in the right direction. The final word is this: don't be afraid to embrace the unknown, stay true to your goals, and always remember that the journey itself is as important as the destination.

You've already begun the most important part of your journey—learning, reflecting, and committing to a meaningful path. Now, it's time to continue evolving, making decisions that align with your values, and building the future you've always dreamed of.

Conclusion

The Advice You Need for a Lifetime of Growth

As we come to the end of this book, it's important to recognize that the advice shared here is not just a one-time fix, but a lifetime toolkit for navigating the evolving journey of your career and personal life. The principles and strategies we've discussed—whether about defining success on your own terms, building relationships, or mastering the art of resilience—are meant to grow with you, not be set aside once you've moved past a chapter.

The truth is, there is no "end" to this journey of self-improvement and career fulfillment. It's a lifelong process, and the tools you've acquired throughout this book are designed to support you in every stage of life—through triumphs, setbacks, transitions, and everything in between.

Embracing the Lifelong Journey of Growth

The most important takeaway is that growth doesn't stop. Even when you achieve success or face challenges, the journey continues. Each moment is an opportunity for growth, refinement, and redefinition. While the world around us may change, one thing remains constant: the need for continuous learning, self-reflection, and adaptation.

As you continue to grow, remember that the foundation you've built is just the beginning. Use what you've learned to fuel your career and life choices, always striving to reach new heights, learn from your experiences, and push your boundaries. The advice within these chapters is meant to inspire action, yes, but also reflection, so you can take each step in your own authentic direction.

Starting Today: Your Path to a Meaningful Life and Career

The journey toward a meaningful career and life starts *right now*. Whether you're just beginning your professional path or are looking for the next chapter in your already established career, there's no better time than today to take action and invest in your future.

Begin With Purpose:

Your career isn't just about what you do, but about why you do it. Start by aligning your career with your values, your passions, and your purpose. Ask yourself:

- What do I truly want to contribute to the world?

- What impact do I want to make through my work?

- How can I ensure that my professional life aligns with who I am at my core?

Take Action:

The most important thing you can do is take action. It doesn't have to be perfect, but it has to be something. Set small, actionable steps today that align with your long-term goals. Whether it's building a new skill, reaching out to a mentor, or simply refining your current goals, action propels you forward.

Remember, It's a Marathon, Not a Sprint:

Building a meaningful life and career is not a race. It's a marathon. Stay patient with yourself as you pursue your goals, and be open to adjusting your path as you learn. Progress doesn't always look linear, and sometimes it's the detours that lead to the greatest discoveries.

Stay Open to Change and Adaptation:

The world will keep evolving, and so should you. As you move through your career, there will be times when you'll need to pivot, adapt, and grow. Embrace the opportunities that come your way, and recognize that change is not only inevitable, but also an essential part of your growth.

A Final Thought

Above all else, remember that the career and life you're building are reflections of your choices, actions, and mindset. You have the power to shape your future, one decision at a time. Use the advice here as a guide, but also trust your intuition, your experiences, and your vision for what you want to accomplish.

This book has equipped you with tools to navigate challenges, seize opportunities, and build a career and life that are meaningful to you. But now, it's up to you to take the next step. To keep evolving. To stay true to your goals. To never stop striving for more, knowing that your best self is always just ahead.

So, take a deep breath, look ahead, and start today. Your journey to a meaningful life and career begins now.

Made in United States
North Haven, CT
10 May 2025

68713837R00055